Dear Parent:
Your child's love of reading starts here!

Every child learns to read in a different way and at his or her own speed. Some go back and forth between reading levels and read favorite books again and again. Others read through each level in order. You can help your young reader improve and become more confident by encouraging his or her own interests and abilities. From books your child reads with you to the first books he or she reads alone, there are I Can Read Books for every stage of reading:

SHARED READING
Basic language, word repetition, and whimsical illustrations, ideal for sharing with your emergent reader

BEGINNING READING
Short sentences, familiar words, and simple concepts for children eager to read on their own

READING WITH HELP
Engaging stories, longer sentences, and language play for developing readers

READING ALONE
Complex plots, challenging vocabulary, and high-interest topics for the independent reader

I Can Read Books have introduced children to the joy of reading since 1957. Featuring award-winning authors and illustrators and a fabulous cast of beloved characters, I Can Read Books set the standard for beginning readers.

A lifetime of discovery begins with the magical words "I Can Read!"

*Visit www.icanread.com for information
on enriching your child's reading experience.*

This book is for everyone who helps keep oceans and beaches clean for sea turtles around the world.
—J.B.

The National Wildlife Federation & Ranger Rick contributors: Children's Publication Staff, Licensing Staff, and in-house naturalist David Mizejewski

I Can Read® and I Can Read Book® are trademarks of HarperCollins Publishers.

Ranger Rick: I Wish I Was a Sea Turtle
Copyright © 2020 National Wildlife Federation. All rights reserved.
Printed in the U.S.A. No part of this book may be used or reproduced in any manner whatsoever without written permission except in the case of brief quotations embodied in critical articles and reviews. For information address HarperCollins Children's Books, a division of HarperCollins Publishers, 195 Broadway, New York, NY 10007.
www.icanread.com
www.RangerRick.com

Library of Congress Control Number: 2019955930
ISBN 978-0-06-243232-2 (trade bdg.) —ISBN 978-0-06-243231-5 (pbk.)

Book design by Brenda E. Angelilli
21 22 23 24 CWM 10 9 8 7 6 5 4   ❖   First Edition

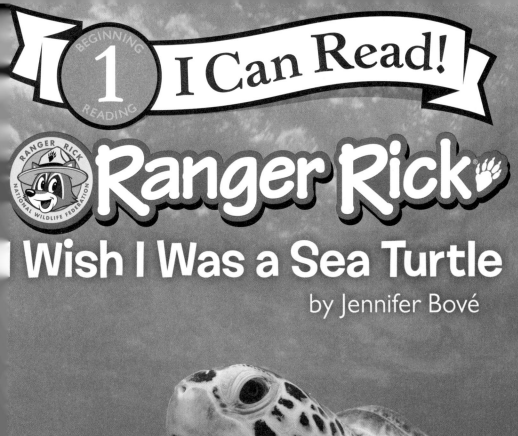

Ranger Rick

I Wish I Was a Sea Turtle

by Jennifer Bové

HARPER

An Imprint of HarperCollinsPublishers

What if you wished you were
a sea turtle?

Then you became a green sea turtle.

Could you swim like a sea turtle?

Eat like a sea turtle?

Spend most of your life underwater?

And would you want to? Find out!

Where would you live?

Green sea turtles live

in warm oceans around the world.

They live underwater,

except when it is time to lay eggs.

Mother turtles leave the water
to lay their eggs on sandy beaches.

Have you ever
visited an ocean?

How would your life begin?

A mother sea turtle clears away
sand with her front flippers
and digs a hole
with her back flippers.

This hole is a nest where she lays
about one hundred eggs.

The mother sea turtle
covers the eggs with sand
and goes back to the ocean.
Sand hides the eggs
from hungry animals.

Two months later, the eggs hatch.

The baby turtles wiggle

their way out of the sand.

Baby turtles are called hatchlings.

When hatchlings leave the nest,

they race toward the ocean

as fast as their flippers will go.

Tiny turtles are not safe on land.
Gulls and other sea birds
might catch them.

Where would you go?

Baby sea turtles
swim way out into the ocean.
They live far from land.
When the sea turtles get bigger,
they move to shallow water
near ocean shores.

How would you breathe?

Sea turtles live underwater,

but they need to breathe air.

They stick their faces

out of the water to breathe.

When sea turtles are sleeping,
they can stay underwater
for five hours
without taking a breath!

Can you hold your
breath underwater?

Where would you sleep?

Sea turtles sleep underwater.

Sometimes they nap while floating.

Sea turtles tuck themselves
under rock ledges
to sleep safely at night.

What would you eat?

Green sea turtles eat seagrasses, seaweed, and other plants that grow in the ocean. Their sharp beaks help them eat these plants.

Have you ever eaten seaweed?

How would you wash up?

Sea turtles do not get dirty.

But plants grow on their shells

and tiny bugs crawl on their skin.

Those things can be itchy!

Fish nibble off the bugs and plants.

Their nibbling helps keep

sea turtles clean and comfortable.

How would growing up change you?

Green sea turtles are fully grown when they are twenty years old. Then they are ready for migration.

Migration means that turtles paddle hundreds of miles back to the same beaches where they hatched.

Sea turtles migrate to find mates.
The female turtles lay eggs.
Then all the adult turtles
swim back to the places
where they can find
their favorite foods.

Have you ever been
far from home?

Being a sea turtle could be cool.

But do you want to live underwater?

Get nibbled clean by fish?

Swim for hundreds of miles?

Luckily, you don't have to.

You're not a sea turtle.

You're YOU!

Did You Know?

- This book is about the green sea turtle. There are six other kinds of sea turtles, too.

- The biggest kind is the leatherback sea turtle, which can weigh over 1,000 pounds.

- The loggerhead sea turtle has a strong beak to crush the hard shells of clams and crabs.

- The hawksbill sea turtle has a beautiful pattern on its shell.

- Sea turtles can live for over fifty years.

Fun Zone

Scientists learn a lot about animals by studying their behavior, or the way they act. What have you learned about sea turtle behavior in this book? Play a game of sea turtle charades to find out. Gather one or two friends. Cut out six squares of paper. Write these turtle behaviors on the squares:

Digging a nest with flippers

Hatching from an egg

Crawling from nest to ocean

Sleeping under a rocky shelf

Eating seagrass

Migrating (paddling for many miles)

Fold the squares and place them in a container. Take turns drawing a paper from the container and acting out the turtle behavior (without talking) in front of your friends until someone guesses correctly.

Wild Words

Flippers: paddle-shaped arms and legs

Hatchling: a turtle that has recently hatched from an egg

Migration: traveling a long distance to nesting and feeding areas

Nest: a hole in the sand where a mother sea turtle lays eggs

Sea turtle: a turtle that lives in the ocean

Seagrass: a grass-like plant that grows in the ocean

Dig Deeper
WANT TO FIND OUT EVEN MORE ABOUT SEA TURTLES?

Check out the Ranger Rick website: www.RangerRick.com
SEARCH: sea turtle

Photography © Getty Images by M. M. Sweet, M Swiet Productions, Sukikaki, g-2-b, kjorgen, I love Photo and Apple, davidevison, ShaneMyersPhoto, Richard Ketai, Chalabala, Greg Sullavan, JHVEPhoto, Nigel Marsh, drewsulockcreations, James Kelley